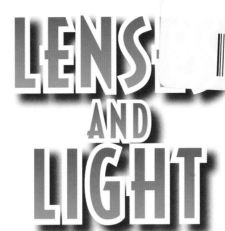

Contents

Rigby
A Harcourt Achieve Imprint

www.Rigby.com
1-800-531-5015

(LENSES AND LIGHT)

Do you know what eyes, telescopes, and cameras have in common? They all have lenses, and they all need light to work properly. In this book, you'll learn how lenses and light work together. You'll also learn how lenses and light affect our lives.

For hundreds of years, people have been using light and lenses to make tiny things look large, to make distant objects seem near, and to improve their vision. Using light and lenses has helped us learn more about life on Earth and about outer space, and it has saved millions of lives.

These three objects, the telescope, camera, and eye, all use lenses and light to do their work.

Long ago, people were curious about where light came from. Plato, a Greek **philosopher** who lived from 427 B.C. to 347 B.C., believed that rays of light came from our eyes. Many of Plato's ideas are still respected today, but this one proved to be incorrect. Plato began the study of light and how it works.

In 280 B.C., a Greek mathematician named Euclid demonstrated that light travels in a straight line. He also developed the law of **reflection**, describing how light bounces off an object. The law said that when a ray of light hits a surface at an angle, it will bounce away at the same angle. If a ray of light hits a surface straight on, it will bounce straight back. Euclid, like Plato, also believed that light came from our eyes, so he wasn't always correct.

How Light Reflects

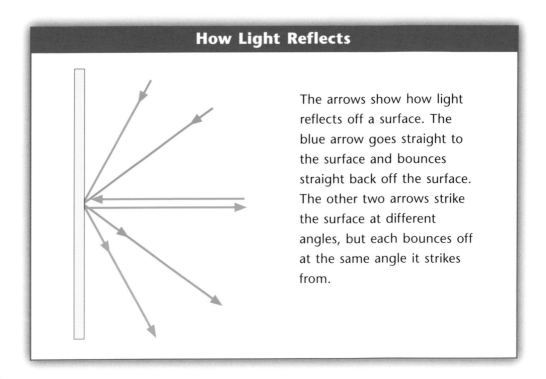

The arrows show how light reflects off a surface. The blue arrow goes straight to the surface and bounces straight back off the surface. The other two arrows strike the surface at different angles, but each bounces off at the same angle it strikes from.

Around 1000 A.D., the Islamic scientist and scholar Alhazen experimented with light. Using mirrors and lenses, he proved that light always travels in a straight line. This supported Euclid's theory. More importantly, perhaps, Alhazen proved that light entered *into* the eye from an outside source. It did not come *from* the eye as Plato and Euclid had thought.

Euclid contributed to the world of mathematics as well as science. He wrote about geometry in a series of 13 books called *Elements*. This series has been studied for 24 centuries in many languages. Today, many people still study Euclidean geometry.

HOW LIGHT ACTS

Since the days of Plato, Euclid, and Alhazen, scientists and mathematicians have learned much about light. They have learned that light is a form of energy that moves in waves, like the water in the ocean. Light is made up of the colors of the rainbow, which combine to make the white or yellowish color we call "light." You can see the rainbow colors after a storm when the sun is shining through the mist and the sunlight splits into its basic colors.

Light acts in certain ways, called **properties**. Some of them you already know. If you look at a light bulb, you know that the light shines in all directions. You also know that if someone gets between a light and a wall, the light makes a shadow because it can't shine through the person.

You already know that light travels in a straight line because you can look at a beam of light at night and see the line it makes. You probably also know that light travels fast. If someone turns on a bright light at the top of a hill that is miles from where you live, you can see the light almost the moment it's turned on. That's because light travels about 186,000 miles a second! You know you can feel light by putting your hand near a light bulb or other source of light. Hold your hand too close or for too long, and it's sure to get very warm.

The light from this beam demonstrates two properties about how light travels. Do you know what they are?

Answer: 1. Light travels in a straight line. 2. Light travels very fast.

In summary, the properties of light you already know are these:
- Light shines in all directions.
- Light can make shadows.
- Light can be felt.
- Light travels very fast.
- Light travels in a straight line.

You're off to a really great start! now it's time to learn more about some properties you may not know very well.

This girl knows that light makes shadows. Have you ever seen people make shadows on the wall like this? They can make the shadows look like animals or monsters and tell stories about them.

ABSORPTION, REFLECTION, AND REFRACTION

When light waves hit any object, three things can happen. The light can be soaked up by the object, it can be bounced back from the object, or it can shine through the object. These three events depend on whether the object is opaque, translucent, or transparent.

All objects let some of the light that hits them bounce back. That is how you see the object. When you look at a friend, what you see is the light bouncing off your friend and going to your eyes. In a totally dark room, no light bounces back from any surface, so you see nothing.

Light waves bounce off these people and onto the sculpture. Then the light waves bounce off the sculpture so the people can see themselves.

An opaque object is one you cannot see through. When light hits an opaque object, most of it is soaked up and only some of the light bounces back. Opaque objects include cars, boats, chairs, tables, books, shoes, and everything else that people can't see through—including you! Did you know that you are opaque?

A shoe is opaque.

A translucent object is one you can almost see through or you can only partly see through. Think of waxed paper, a stained glass window, thin curtains, some drinking glasses, and some types of plastic. Translucent objects soak up some light, let some of it bounce back, and let much of the light shine through.

Stained glass is usually translucent.

Transparent objects let most of the light that hits them shine through. These objects include windows, some drinking glasses, and water.

This glass is transparent.

Absorption: Light That Is Soaked Up

If you spill some water, you might grab a bunch of paper towels to soak it up, or absorb it. Light is absorbed by objects just like a paper towel absorbs water. Remember that opaque objects, like phones and books, absorb more light than translucent or transparent objects. The darker the object, the more light it absorbs. That's why some people who live where it gets very hot want white cars instead of black ones. White cars don't absorb as much sunlight and heat as black cars do. Absorption is a property of light.

All objects absorb light like this paper towel is absorbing colored water from the egg. Right now you are absorbing light or you wouldn't be able to read this book!

Reflection: Light That Bounces Back

When light bounces off an object, it is called reflection. You can see your face reflected in a mirror. When you ride down the street, you can often see clouds and the sky reflected in the glass of office buildings. When you look at a shiny new car, you can often see objects reflected in it.

A smooth object, like a mirror or a shiny car, reflects light back so you can see the reflection clearly. A rough object, on the other hand, causes the reflection to scatter in different directions. Reflection is a property of light.

The mirror and the shiny car are objects that reflect most of the light that strikes them.

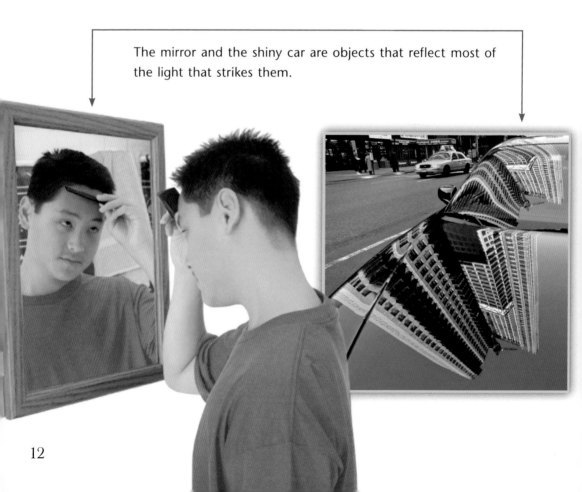

Refraction: Light That Bends

If light strikes a window or a clear glass, it passes right through and you can see exactly what is on the other side of the glass. That's because the glass is transparent and smooth. Light takes a straight path through the glass and does not scatter.

If you put water into a clear glass and then you drop in a marble, the marble might look like it's broken or lopsided. This happens when light shines through one material (glass) and then through a different material (water). The light doesn't go straight through. It bends and scatters. This is called refraction.

Because the glass is transparent, the girl is able to look through it.

Refraction comes from the Latin word *refractus,* which means to break. The pencil in the water in this glass looks like it's broken.

13

A VERY CLEVER FISH

Archerfish hunt in a most unusual way. They feed on insects that sit on branches just above the water's surface. If the insect is close, they jump for it. Otherwise, archerfish are known for knocking their prey into the water by squirting a strong stream of water out of their mouths. They are named archerfish because they get their prey much like an archer does using an arrow.

The archerfish spits from a groove at the top of its mouth. It puts its tongue below the groove to form a tube, and then it snaps its gills shut very quickly to make a stream of water that can shoot 6–8 feet in the air. The tip of the fish's tongue helps it aim the jet of water. The water hits the prey, the prey drops into the water, and the archerfish waits with its mouth open.

To the archerfish looking up through the water, refraction makes the insects appear to be in places they are not really in. Archerfish must be able to work out where the insect actually is so they know exactly where to aim.

Amazingly, archerfish have learned to swim directly under the insect to get the best shooting spot. Here it is easier to see the insect because there is less refraction.

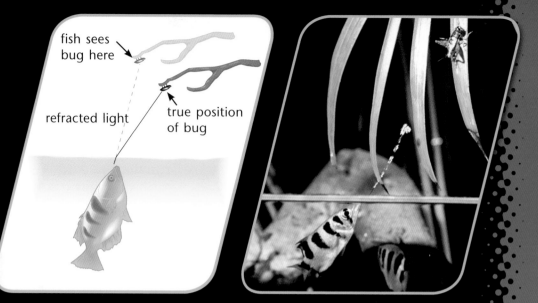

fish sees bug here

refracted light

true position of bug

The insect isn't where it appears to be when the archerfish looks at it. This is because of refraction when the light moves from the water to the air.

unrefracted light

The archerfish is looking at the insect in a straight line, so there is little or no refraction.

You should now be able to demonstrate what you know about how light acts. When someone sees a reflection of something like clouds or other buildings in the windows of a skyscraper, you can explain that smooth surfaces like windows cause light to bounce back evenly, making reflections. People on the inside of a window can see out clearly because the windows are transparent and almost all light goes through them.

Light works in very specific and known ways. This means scientists know how to create **solutions** that use light, and they can predict how those solutions will work. They know exactly how to use different types of materials to reflect, absorb, or refract light in just the right way. That's what the next part of this book is about. You'll see how light is combined with lenses, mirrors, and other objects to make telescopes, microscopes, cameras, and other important tools. You'll even get to make your own telescope, periscope, and camera!

From the inside, most light goes through the window on the left. From the outside, most light reflects off the glass building on the right.

LENSES

Lenses can make small items look larger and distant objects look nearer. Today, we use magnifying glasses to read small objects, like maps, and eyeglasses to help us read and see in the distance. Both types of glasses use lenses.

Zacharius Jensen created the first microscope in 1570. Jensen's microscope had two lenses as did the first telescope developed by Hans Lippershey in 1608. The next year Galileo built his own telescope, using Lippershey's design, and began to study the skies. Galileo discovered that the moon had huge craters, Jupiter had four moons, and Venus had phases like our moon. These discoveries, made possible by a simple telescope, convinced Galileo that the earth and other planets revolve around the sun.

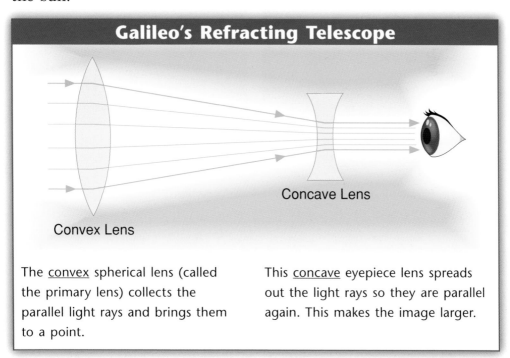

Galileo's Refracting Telescope

Concave Lens

Convex Lens

The <u>convex</u> spherical lens (called the primary lens) collects the parallel light rays and brings them to a point.

This <u>concave</u> eyepiece lens spreads out the light rays so they are parallel again. This makes the image larger.

Kinds of Lenses

There are two kinds of lenses: convex and concave. Both types use a combination of reflection and refraction to make an image seem larger.

1. A convex lens curves outward. The edges are thin and the center is wide. A convex lens used alone makes objects look larger and, often, a little blurry.

2. A concave lens curves inward. The edges are wide and the center is thin. A concave lens used alone makes objects look clear but small.

These lenses are used in microscopes, telescopes, eyeglasses, contact lenses, and many other objects.

Convex Lens	Concave Lens
Thick in the middle, thin at the edge.	Thick at the edges, thin in the middle.
Refracts parallel light rays so they come together at a single point.	Refracts light rays so they spread apart and become parallel.

USING LENSES

Using a convex lens, try to read a newspaper or a book. Hold the lens close to your eye. Can you see the writing clearly? Now move it farther away. How does it change what you see?

If you hold the lens close to your eye, the image you see through it should be right-side up and larger than the actual text. If you hold the lens farther away, the image will appear to be upside down.

Hold a concave lens close to your eye. You will see images right-side up and smaller than they actually are. Now look through the lens at the words in a book. Can you see the writing clearly? Move the lens closer to your eye. Now move it farther away. Does this change what you see?

This boy is exploring with his convex magnifying glass. It lets him see many small objects that he would have trouble seeing without it.

MAGNIFICATION

Magnification means making something small look big. Lucius Seneca, who lived from 5 B.C. to 65 A.D., was the first to write about how liquids magnified the appearance of objects in clear containers. As scientists learned more about light and lenses, they realized that looking at an object through a convex lens magnified it, or made it look bigger. So they used convex lenses to create magnifying glasses.

This magnifying glass is being held over a flower and makes the flower seem larger. Do you think this magnifying glass has a concave or convex lense?

Answer: The lens is convex.

Flea Glasses and Microscopes

Scientists wanted to look at very small things such as fleas and other insects and needed more powerful convex lenses. When the simple microscope was developed—an instrument with powerful lenses that made objects look bigger—people used it to study fleas. The microscope became known as "flea glasses."

In the early to mid-1600s, Anton van Leeuwenhoek (Lay-vun-hook) learned how to grind and polish these flea glasses to make them more powerful. He built a microscope that allowed him to see and describe **bacteria**, plant **tissue**, and other things that could not be seen by human eyes alone. Most of the things Leeuwenhoek studied were smaller than the period at the end of this sentence.

This person is using a model of the simple microscope invented by van Leeuwenhoek. A convex lens has been placed in a small hole in the brass plate. The object being viewed has been pinned to the pointed tip, and the screws can be moved to put the object in front of the lens.

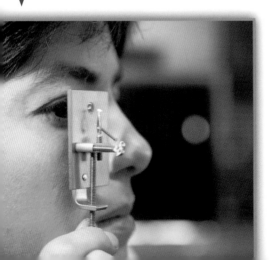

This is a magnified flea. People were so interested in looking at fleas that the first simple microscopes were called "flea glasses."

Around the same time that van Leeuwenhoek was doing his work, the Janssen brothers and Galileo made compound microscopes, meaning they used two convex lenses. Galileo called one the **objective** lens and the other the **ocular** lens. The objective lens reflected a larger picture of an object into the tube. Then the ocular lens, which was close to the person's eye, made the picture inside the tube look even bigger.

This is a brass copy of one of Galileo's early compound microscopes. The original microscope was made of cardboard, leather, and wood.

Galileo Galilei, 1564–1642

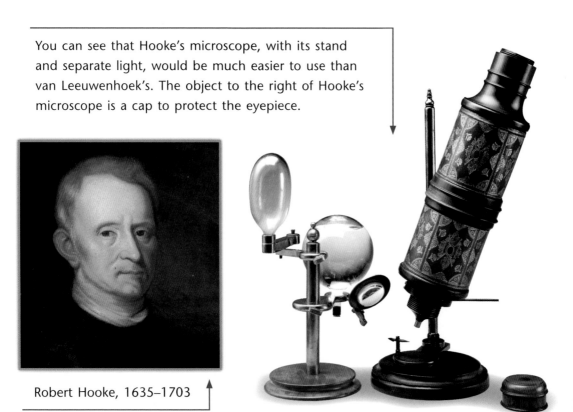

You can see that Hooke's microscope, with its stand and separate light, would be much easier to use than van Leeuwenhoek's. The object to the right of Hooke's microscope is a cap to protect the eyepiece.

Robert Hooke, 1635–1703

A British scientist named Robert Hooke also created a compound microscope. Hooke's microscope had its own light that let him see smaller objects more easily. This light enabled Hooke to become the first person to study plant and animal cells.

Hooke's compound microscope made objects look 20 to 30 times bigger than they were, but van Leeuwenhoek's simple microscope made things look as much as 300 times bigger. The compound microscopes at that time were more comfortable than van Leeuwenhoek's, which was tiring and difficult to use. However, at that time, no other microscope was more powerful than van Leeuwenhoek's.

Modern Compound Microscopes

A modern compound microscope works much like Hooke's microscope made in the 1600s. In a modern compound microscope, the **specimen** is clipped to the flat area above the viewing hole. Light is aimed at a mirror on the bottom of the microscope. Then this light is reflected up through the hole and onto the object. The objective lens reflects an image of the specimen up into the body tube. The eyepiece, or ocular lens, makes the image look even bigger.

Modern microscopes usually have two or three objective lenses to magnify an object. The lenses are often made of glass. A number on the lens tells us how large it will make the specimen appear. For example, if it says *30X*, the specimen will appear 30 times larger than its actual size.

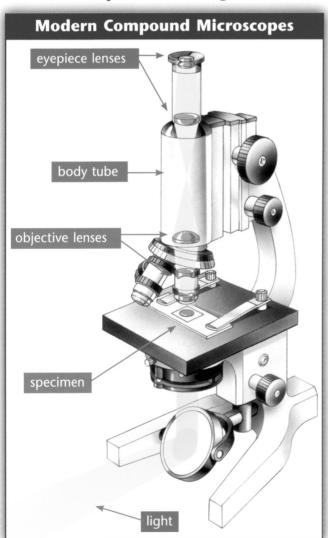

Modern Compound Microscopes

eyepiece lenses

body tube

objective lenses

specimen

light

TRY IT!

MAKING A LENS WITH WATER

You can make your own water drop lens and use it to magnify the appearance of a stamp. You'll need:

- see-through sticky tape
- a small cup of water
- an eyedropper
- a used postage stamp
- plastic wrap
- a small plate

1. Tape the stamp to the bottom of the plate.
2. Cover the plate with enough plastic wrap to keep the stamp from getting wet.
3. Use the eyedropper to place a drop of water above the stamp.
4. Look at the stamp through the water. How does it look now? What type of lens does the drop of water remind you of?

For a fun experiment, make a prediction about how the appearance of the stamp will change if you add more (or less) water. Record your answers and share them with your class.

Water can do many things. We drink it, we wash with it, we water our plants with it. It can even magnify, as you can see by observing how the drops of rain have enlarged parts of this feather. What an amazing substance!

TELESCOPES

We can't see objects that are very far away because our eyes can't capture enough light to see the details. If we had much bigger eyes, we could gather more light from the object and see a better image of it.

Telescopes are tubes with lenses that magnify objects from far away. They make it possible for us to have "bigger eyes." They pull in more light to create a brighter image, and then they magnify the image.

Light enters the telescope from the larger end of the tube, and an image is created. We look through an eyepiece, which magnifies that image so more of the image and light hit our eyes. Now we can see details of far away objects we never dreamed we'd see before!

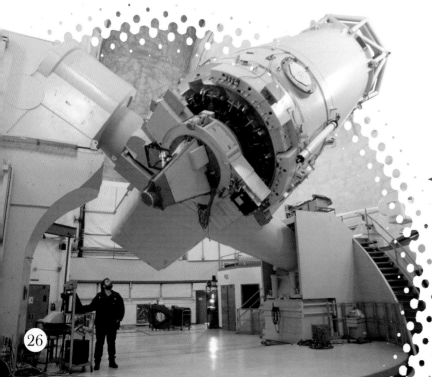

This large telescope allows scientists to look far out into space. Scientists collect information from the telescope by using computers and taking digital pictures.

Types of Telescopes

There are two types of telescopes: those that refract and those that reflect. A basic refracting telescope is a tube with two convex lenses, one at each end. Convex lenses can make images appear large but blurry, so refracting telescopes may also use a convex lens that is combined with a concave lens. With longer tubes and larger lenses, refracting telescopes pick up details from far away.

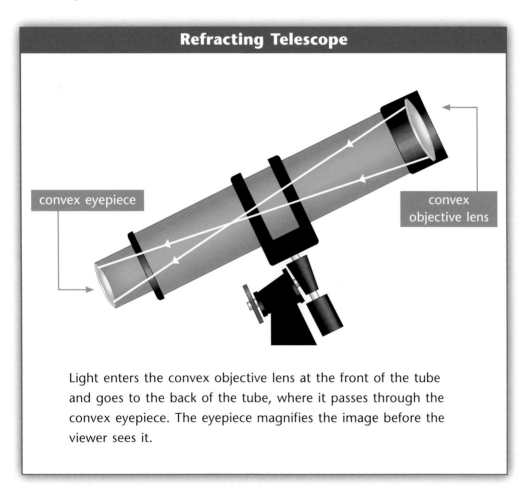

Refracting Telescope

convex eyepiece

convex objective lens

Light enters the convex objective lens at the front of the tube and goes to the back of the tube, where it passes through the convex eyepiece. The eyepiece magnifies the image before the viewer sees it.

The Spyglass While many people used lenses to make small things look big, others used lenses to make faraway objects seem close. In the early 1600s, Hans Lippershey, a German man who made eyeglasses, created a simple instrument to look at objects that were far from Earth. He called it a spyglass.

He made the spyglass by placing a tube between two lenses. Some people think he got the idea while watching his children playing in his shop. They held up two lenses to their eyes and when they looked through them, the children could clearly see a weathervane that was very far away.

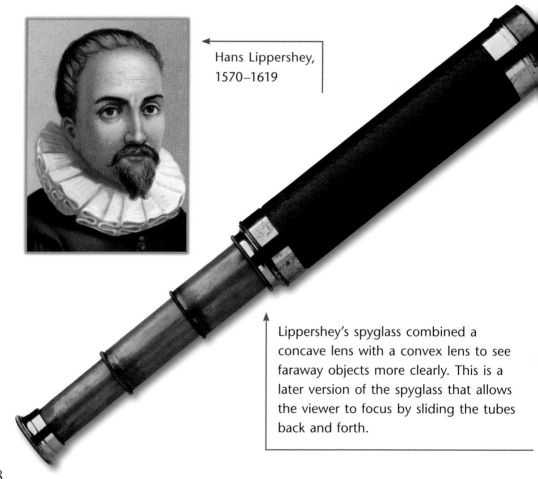

Hans Lippershey,
1570–1619

Lippershey's spyglass combined a concave lens with a convex lens to see faraway objects more clearly. This is a later version of the spyglass that allows the viewer to focus by sliding the tubes back and forth.

The First Refracting Telescope When Galileo heard that Lippershey invented a spyglass, he wanted to build one, too. So in 1609, he made his first refracting telescope, using a convex lens at the end of the tube and a concave lens for the eyepiece lens.

Galileo used this telescope to look at objects in the sky. He discovered that the moon had a rough, rocky surface, not a smooth one as everyone believed during that time. He also discovered that the planet Jupiter had four moons like Earth's moon. These discoveries convinced Galileo that the Earth and other planets revolve, or take a path around, the sun.

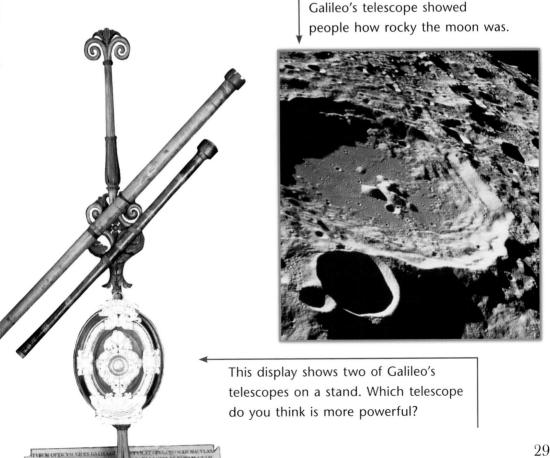

Galileo's telescope showed people how rocky the moon was.

This display shows two of Galileo's telescopes on a stand. Which telescope do you think is more powerful?

TRY IT!

MAKE A GALILEAN TELESCOPE

You can make your own telescope like the one Galileo made. You'll need:

- Lens A: concave lens
- two clothespins
- Lens B: convex lens

Tip: Make sure your lenses are labeled before you begin this project.

Directions:

1. Place a pencil on a desk. Then move to the other side of the room.

2. Clamp the edge of each lens with a clothespin. Hold Lens A extremely close to your eye, so that it almost touches your eyebrow.

3. Hold Lens B right in front of it, so when you look through Lens A, you are also looking through Lens B.

4. Close your other eye.

5. Look at the pencil through Lens A. Keep the lens close to your eye. Move Lens B farther from Lens A until you can see the pencil clearly.

6. Draw a picture of your pencil at the size it appears when you look at it through the lenses; then draw a picture of your pencil at the size it appears when you look at it without using the lenses.

7. Measure the length of the pencil in each drawing. Divide the larger number by the smaller number, and this will give you the magnification of your telescope.

The First Reflecting Telescope The major problem with Lippershey's spyglass and Galileo's telescope was that the image quality was blurry. Isaac Newton addressed the problem around the year 1670 by inventing the first reflecting telescope. He replaced the convex lens with a curved mirror. Instead of light passing through the lens, it now reflected off the mirror. This focused the light and removed the rings of color that once made the images blurry. It also made telescopes shorter and easier to work with. Although it wasn't perfect at the time, Newton's design is used in optical telescopes today.

Isaac Newton began another new trend in telescope design. He added another mirror inside his telescope so his head wouldn't block the light as he looked inside the instrument. The lens reflected the light through the side of the telescope.

Reflecting Telescope

Light comes in through the large opening in the tube and goes to a big concave mirror at the back of the tube. This mirror reflects the image to a smaller mirror, which in turn reflects it into the eyepiece. The eyepiece magnifies the image even more and makes it easier for the viewer to see.

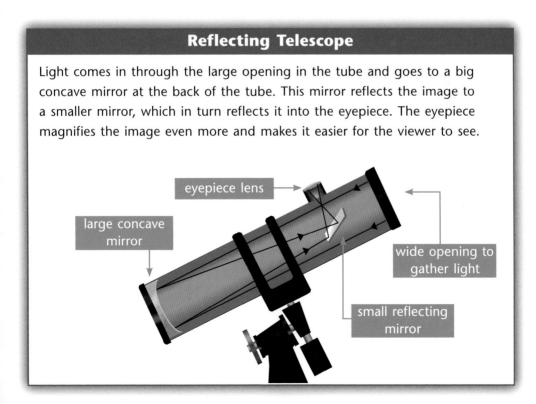

eyepiece lens

large concave mirror

wide opening to gather light

small reflecting mirror

Early refracting telescopes produced a blurry image because the lenses were bending colors at different angles. Today refracting telescopes are seldom used for astronomy because of their poor light-gathering ability. Reflecting telescopes were developed to eliminate this problem. Instead of lenses, reflecting telescopes rely on mirrors. Most of the largest telescopes, like the Hubble, are reflecting rather than refracting telescopes mainly because it is easier to build and maintain large high-quality mirrors than it is to develop and support large lenses.

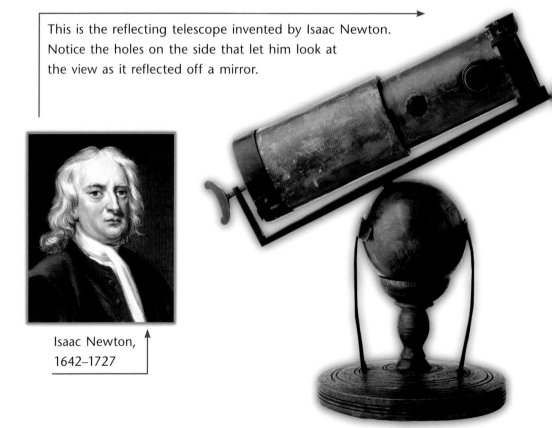

This is the reflecting telescope invented by Isaac Newton. Notice the holes on the side that let him look at the view as it reflected off a mirror.

Isaac Newton, 1642–1727

The Hubble Space Telescope The Hubble Space Telescope has been floating 380 miles above the earth since its launch in 1990. It sends back enormous amounts of data to the earth each day.

The Hubble telescope weighs more than 12 tons and is about the size of a large school bus. It circles the earth every 97 minutes and gets its power from two solar panels, each 25 feet long. Hubble's main mirror is almost 8 feet across and weighs 1,825 pounds. It was smoothed and polished to be an almost perfect curve.

Hubble's mission is to explore the solar system, measure the age and size of the universe, and unlock the mysteries of galaxies, stars, and planets. That is asking a lot, but Hubble has done a wonderful job of performing its duties. It has taken photos that confirm the birth of new planets around newborn stars. It showed a place where stars are born. And it found more than 1,500 galaxies not seen before.

The Hubble Space Telescope took this image of an exploding star in December 2002. The circle that looks like clouds around the star is a layer of dust from earlier explosions.

A VERY
CLEVER TELESCOPE

Hubble doesn't transmit picture images back to Earth. Instead it focuses onto photoelectric sensors, which convert the images into digital signals — basically, a set of numbers — through the use of a computer. The numbers are transmitted by radio back to Earth to a second computer, which decodes the signals and reassembles the numbers into a spectacular image from space.

TRY IT!

SEEING AROUND CORNERS AND ABOVE THE WATER

For years submarines have patrolled under water, guarding the shores. Long ago, sailors on subs had been unable to see where they were without coming out of the water, which could be dangerous. Then, in the mid-1800s, the first "sight tube" or "optical tube" was built. It had two flat mirrors at 45-degree angles that faced opposite directions inside the tube. Sailors were able to see a small area above sea level using this sight tube.

Why do you think the "sight tube" used two mirrors? This simple exercise might help you find the answer.

1. Look into a mirror. What do you see? Of course, you see your reflection — and the image of you is reversed!

2. Now turn your back to the mirror.

3. Hold up a small mirror in front of you and use it to look into the mirror that is now behind you.

Describe the image of you. Is it still reversed? Think about how using two mirrors instead of one might help a submarine crew under the water.

This man is using a periscope to look over the heads of people in the crowd.

35

HELPING PEOPLE SEE

The eye is a complex organ that is able to adjust so we can see objects near or distant. The cornea is a thin, transparent tissue that covers the eye to protect it. The cornea also refracts, or bends, light that enters the eye. Behind the cornea is a small amount of fluid, the same kind that fills the eyeball, and behind that small bit of fluid is the lens of the eye. The lens is made of a jelly-like, transparent substance that also refracts light. It is connected to two small muscles, called ciliary muscles.

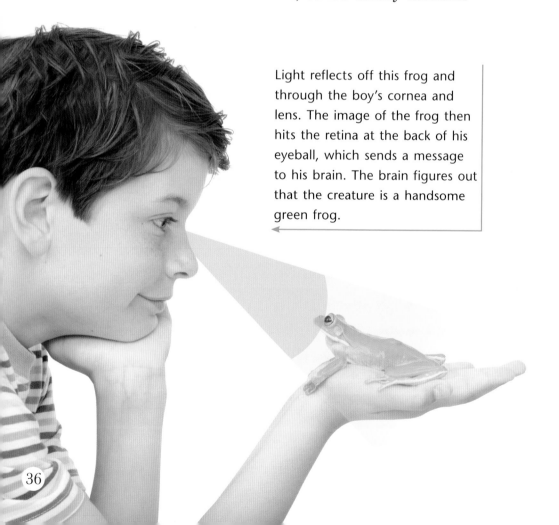

Light reflects off this frog and through the boy's cornea and lens. The image of the frog then hits the retina at the back of his eyeball, which sends a message to his brain. The brain figures out that the creature is a handsome green frog.

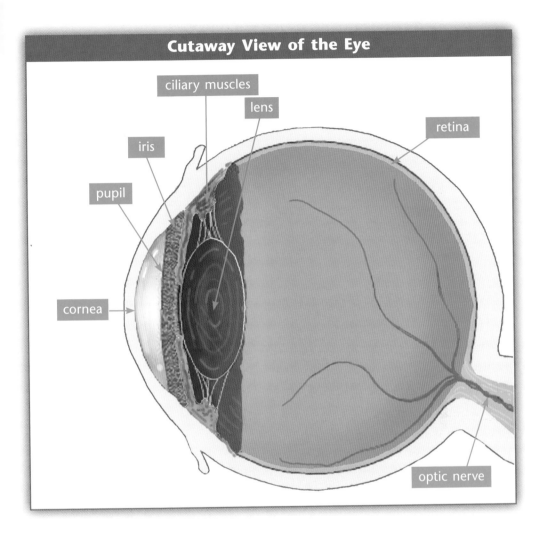

Cutaway View of the Eye

ciliary muscles

lens

retina

iris

pupil

cornea

optic nerve

When you look at something, the ciliary muscles tighten or relax to change the shape of the lens. The way the lens is shaped affects the refraction of the light coming into the eye. It is very important that the light hits an exact spot on the back of the eyeball, called the retina, because the retina sends a signal to the brain through the optic nerve. Then the brain figures out what you are seeing.

The most common eye problems people suffer are nearsightedness and farsightedness, where the image strikes in front of the retina or behind it. Sometimes the vision problem is caused by a lens or cornea that is not perfectly shaped, and other times it is due to the shape of the eyeball.

Nearsightedness means you can see objects that are near but not those that are far away. The cornea may bulge too much or the eyeball may be a bit too long. This causes the image to focus in front of the retina, as in the figure below. The millions of rods and cones on the surface of the retina see the image, but it is fuzzy to them. So they send a fuzzy image to the brain.

To correct for nearsightedness, the eye needs to have less refraction. In other words, it needs to spread out a bit before it strikes the cornea so the focus won't be too short. The figure below shows how a concave lens causes the light to spread out so that when it passes through the cornea and lens, it strikes the correct spot on the retina.

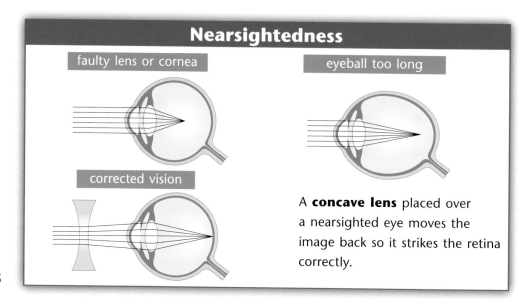

Nearsightedness

faulty lens or cornea

eyeball too long

corrected vision

A **concave lens** placed over a nearsighted eye moves the image back so it strikes the retina correctly.

The opposite happens with farsightedness, where you can see clearly objects that are far away but not those up close, such as a map or movie. This problem often happens as you get older and the ciliary muscles become weak or the lens becomes less **flexible**. In either case, the lens can't assume the very curved shape needed to direct the images to the correct spot on the retina. Instead they focus behind the retina, and once again, a blurry image is sent to the brain.

To correct for farsightedness, the eye needs more refraction. The light from the image needs to come closer together before it strikes the cornea. A convex lens makes the light refract more so it strikes the retina correctly.

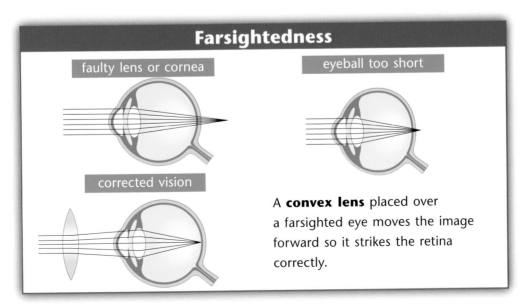

Farsightedness

faulty lens or cornea

eyeball too short

corrected vision

A **convex lens** placed over a farsighted eye moves the image forward so it strikes the retina correctly.

BEN FRANKLIN'S
BIFOCAL LENSES

Some people are both nearsighted and farsighted. Benjamin Franklin was both. His contribution to the science of improving vision with lenses was bifocals, with one lens in the bottom half of the glasses and the other lens in the top. When you look at items up close, you usually look down, so that's where the concave lens was. When you look at distant objects, you are usually looking straight ahead, so the convex lens was put at the top.

What's the Latest in Eye Correction?

In about 1267, Roger Bacon discovered that certain lenses made small objects look larger. He suggested that this process could be applied to help people with poor eyesight. Since then, scientists have worked to improve the way people see.

Contact Lenses You probably know someone who wears contact lenses instead of eyeglasses. A glassblower in Germany named F. E. Muller put the first lens in a patient's eye in 1887. The man had lost his eyelid due to disease, and the lens was designed to protect the man's eye rather than to correct his vision. It must have been terribly uncomfortable. The man wore it, however, for 20 years and never lost his sight, so it did work!

Soft contact lenses made of plastic have been available since the 1960s. Some can now be worn overnight, and others can even be worn for two weeks before they need changing. They even come in bifocals.

Doctors are now moving beyond contact lenses and using laser surgery to correct vision. They can reshape the lens of the eye by using a laser to take out tiny slices and change the curve. People who have this surgery can usually see correctly as soon as the procedure is finished.

old contact lens

new contact lens

Artificial Lenses A cataract is a cloudy spot on the lens of the eye that often appears as a person gets older. As it gets worse, the person has trouble seeing or driving at night and, eventually, even in the daytime. When cataracts cause problems, the person can have surgery, where the real lens is removed and an artificial lens is put in. The patient goes home shortly after surgery and is able to see clearly almost immediately.

The same procedure used to repair cataracts can now be done for nearsightedness and farsightedness. Corneas can be transplanted, allowing people who have not seen anything in a long time to see again.

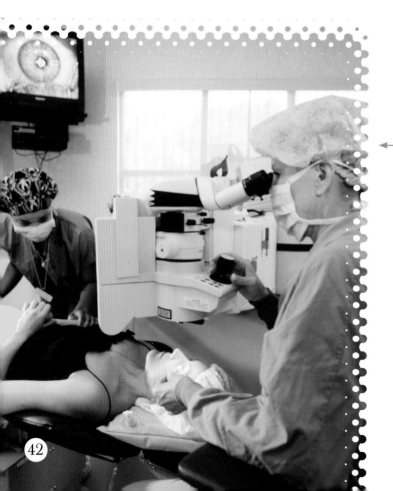

The doctor is using a microscope to enlarge his view of the patient's eye. This allows him to see more details and fine tune his procedure.

CAMERAS

Lenses and light are important in many items we use for entertainment as well as the scientific products discussed so far. This includes projectors, cameras, rear-projection televisions, and periscopes on submarines, to name a few. We'll look at a camera now to see how much of what we've learned about telescopes and microscopes can be applied to cameras.

A camera cannot record an image with only its convex lens—the curved piece of glass or plastic that gathers, focuses, and redirects beams of light that bounce off a subject to record it on film as an image. A camera also needs several key features to work: an aperture, or hole, to let light in, a shutter to control the amount of light that comes into the camera, and film chemicals that react with light to record the image.

Waves of light travel quickly through the air from subject to camera, but when these waves reach the lens, they slow down and bend. Light bends toward the middle of the lens, and its angle depends on how close the camera is to its subject.

Camera Lenses

There are several kinds of camera lenses that have different functions. Zoom lenses are made up of different lens elements that move back and forth, changing the distance, or focal length, between the lens and the subject. Zoom lenses allow people, without moving, to capture a subject in more detail, depending on how much magnification power they want.

Telephoto lenses have a longer focal length to help a photographer capture faraway details in city and nature scenes. A wide-angle lens is a great lens to use for a class photo because it has a shorter focal length that can include many students in the same photograph. These lenses are based on the same principles as the lenses discussed earlier.

wide-angle

regular

zoom

Three different lenses were used to photograph the Statue of Liberty. Notice the way each lens changes how you see the statue.

44

PINHOLE CAMERAS

Did you know you could make your own camera? It's called a pinhole camera. The pinhole camera is a small, light-tight can or box painted black inside and containing a tiny hole in the center of one end. This kind of simple camera doesn't require any kind of lens, but it does need light.

To take pictures, a roll or sheet of film is placed inside the dark box. Light goes through the hole, hits the film, and creates an image. Pinhole cameras, as simple as they are, can take pretty good pictures!

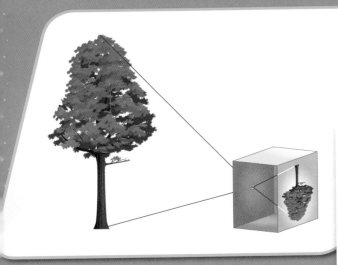

A pinhole camera is very simple. Even though it is simple, it can still take nice pictures, as you can see from this image.

It took more than 2,000 years to move from early questions and discoveries about using light and lenses to the place we find ourselves today. That's a long journey. Think about how long it took to get from 1946, when Dr. Spitzer suggested the Hubble Space Telescope, to launching it into space in 1990. That journey took less than 44 years! As early as 2008, the next-generation space telescope is supposed to be launched. It's the James E. Webb Space Telescope, with a mirror more than 21 feet across and a sunshield the size of a tennis court. That's progress!

Microscopes have become so powerful that we can see the smallest objects we know about. We can look forward to the use of these microscopes in fields like medicine, where they are now capable of finding evidence of disease before the person has any symptoms.

An engineer inspects a telescope for the James E. Webb project launch in 2008.

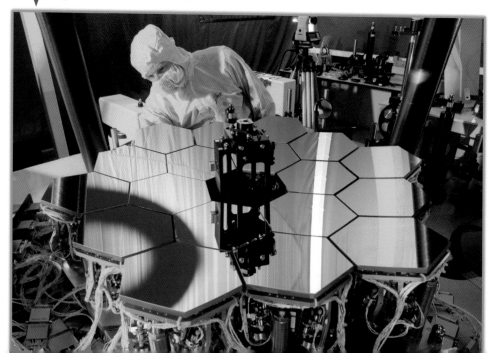

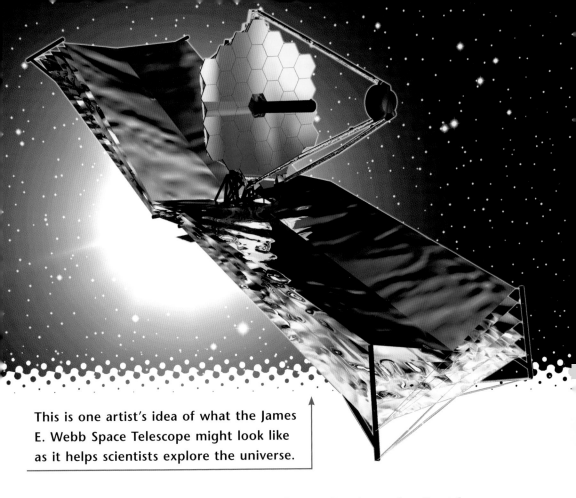

This is one artist's idea of what the James E. Webb Space Telescope might look like as it helps scientists explore the universe.

Vision improvement has changed greatly since the first lens was put in that poor fellow's eye in 1887. Surgery can painlessly improve vision within minutes. Artificial lenses can be placed in the eye. Newer surgeries can help some people who have never been able to see peer at the world around them.

Where might these discoveries go next? In another 50 years, how will we be viewing objects distant or tiny? It's an exciting time for learning about our world. Who knows, you might become a famous optician, astronomer, microbiologist—or work in any of the many fields related to light and lenses. Good luck!

GLOSSARY

bacteria tiny animals; also called organisms

compound something that has more parts and is harder to make and use

flexible able to bend or move easily

objective having to do with the object being studied

ocular having to do with the eye

philosopher someone who studies how people think

properties important qualities about something that help you define or describe it

refraction the bending of a ray of light when it travels from one substance to another

simple something that is easy to make and use; has few parts

specimen something that is being studied or examined

solutions ways to solve problems

tissue a covering, such as skin

INDEX